My Nana Was Demeter

Brittney McKinley

BookLeaf Publishing

India | USA | UK

Presentation by *BookLeaf Publishing*

Web: www.bookleafpub.com

E-mail: info@bookleafpub.com

ISBN:

First edition 2022

DEDICATION

To my Mom

I love you, thank you for always telling me to
write

ACKNOWLEDGEMENT

I have never written an author's note before, and it feels a bit silly. I read every single author's note and dedication I can find, and now it comes time to write one and I'm drawing a blank. I suppose it's because only friends and family will know this book exists, and it feels strange treating you all like an audience I don't know intimately. I hope you enjoyed reading my poetry, I'm very proud of what I created, but I'll be totally honest: I did this more for myself than anyone else. So I'll give an author's note to future me - never forget the pure joy writing this gave you! The words fell out of you faster than you could tap them into your phone screen. I hope you keep this passion and love of writing wherever you go:)

Orpheus

his shirt is drenched in sweat
muscles in his back tighten and release with
every step
a man of song
of lyre
of foolish courage

I cannot see his face
is he smiling, is his brow furrowed
is he staring into the light that twinkles above
is he watching his feet press into the mist and
shadowed rock beneath our feet

I cannot know
so, I watch his back
and through that shirt, into those muscles, I press
my will into him with every step
Don't turn
Don't turn
Don't turn

a sliver of sunlight
traces over my ghostly skin
Apollo's buttery rays weave stripes across my
cheeks

I see the sky, clear and blue
it goes on forever, unbroken

until my eyes clash with a brown I know too
well
my dear, I would know those eyes anywhere
we had but one moment, frozen in time
a great victory turned sour
ambrosia rotting on our tongues

all I can do now is remember
your face in that instant
those brown depths held so much sorrow
convinced beyond reason I would leave you
how could I leave you?

darkness fell
as it always does
and I am left in the grassy plains once more
a world away from you
lost in my slow thoughts
repeating and reliving my last moments with you

your determination
your beautiful song
your doubt
and your eyes

Callisto

callisto hangs above me in the stars
a mother with love made of starlight and
galaxies
she peers down at me
cheeks of Mars eyes of Neptune
and her smile is made of you

I'm stretched across the land
only your voice can reach me here
the echo of a phone call
fuzzy words and star-lit love clambering down
the line

I left our horizon for a new one
charting a life planets away
tracing through inky space in search of nothing
and everything
you celebrate the freedom
but you miss the daughter
I miss you too

but I pray you won't worry
for Callisto watches every daughter here
eyes of Neptune tracing our movements
claws of comets and teeth of moons

keep us safe from harm

she watches me walk down a glittering city
street
she watches me chase dreams and lose them
she watches me fall in love
she watches me become the woman you raised
me to be

and some nights, on that glittering street
I stop and look up
imagine that the city lights are dimmer than the
glow of Callisto's stars
imagine that it's not her eyes up there
but yours
and I imagine you see every little thing

Demeter

my Nana was Demeter
with Titan blood flowing through her veins
she stood so strong and tall, Boreas had no hope
of folding her
she rooted her self in every moment, like the
willow tree in her backyard
soaring defiantly into the sky,
with gentle wisps reaching back down to those
she loved on earth
a pillar and a warmth
as immortal and inevitable as a goddess

my Nana was Demeter
soft grower of all things green
wrists and elbows never leaving the soil
she imbued her garden with ancient magic,
spilling her emerald love into the roots
until every inch of her quiet paradise spilled
vines and leaves
a peaceful hilltop in the clouds, tucked away
a green and living Olympus
where a goddess watched the world roll by
beneath her
armed with a knowing smile and a gardening
shovel

with flowers blooming in her soul
roots twisting in her veins
sunlit green filaments glowing in her gaze

my Nana was Demeter
beautiful and unchanged by mortals
no make up spread across her skin
hair cropped up off her neck
strong muscles under her sun-darkened skin
once a girl with bandaged knees and dirty
cheeks
with no concern for femininity or poise
she roared against tradition
she ran with her titan blood, faster than any man
leaving her mortal playmates in clouds of dust
and gravel
in a time when a woman's place was behind a
man
she sprinted forward at an unstoppable and
unapologetic pace
and later, she sat on every bleacher in glaring
sun or roaring wind
to watch me run with her speed,
gifted through her golden ichor
I ran behind fences that men closed in her face
in her name with her defiance racing through my
heart
she cheered at every victory with the same smile
part rebellion and part pride

my Nana was Demeter
a mother and a nurturer
with the same patience and adoration she grew
plants, she also raised people
first two sons
she pulled them from sacred soil into the world
nursed their roots and misted their leaves
and with every day spent tending their garden
beds
she wove her strength, intelligence, and
boundless love into them
standing strong and eternal as a redwood, her
roots fixed her in time
two blonde boys ran around her
brushing her knees, hips, shoulders, head, and
they were gone into the world
years later, she watched two blonde girls run
those same footsteps
tread the same well-worn path from youth to
adolescence under her shady willow branches
her goddess-mother touch reaching through
generations

my Nana was Demeter
and our Goddess returned to the sky
her time here done
we mortals bear the weight of her departure
heavy upon our shoulders and our hearts

but we see every piece of her left behind
the green of a garden
the brush of a warm summer wind
the unrelenting blue of the sky
the pounding of feet upon a track
the warmth of an embrace
and the strength she grew within all of us

Medusa

I know many women who have gone to visit
Medusa
living in a stone cottage by a lazily winding river
on the edge of a forest somewhere foggy and
almost magical
you make your way across the stones leading to
her cottage
and as you approach
she opens the front door
her figure outlined by the warm light inside

wrists and fingers glimmering with silver
jewelry
draped in a knitted sweater, socked feet on wood
floors
she looks little like a priestess
with her snakes an idle and slow-moving knot
atop her head
their scales rasping quietly against each other

a smile soft and familiar
a hand gentle in yours
kind green eyes faintly glowing
with Athena's curse-gift
you're drawn out of the misty chill

and into the home of this gentle gorgon
a fire flickering in the corner
walls lined with bookshelves surround you
a velvety and overstuffed couch before you
she offers you a cup of tea with too much honey
talk warmly with her, like an old friend
laugh at the bust of a screaming man on her
mantle
she giggles delightedly along with you
yes dear of course he deserved it

the smile slides slowly off of your face
bookshelves slither in your vision
as tears begin to fall
silent and burning
fingers clutching the velvet beneath you
her eyebrows crease with concern and
understanding
she knows what brought you to her, after all

heroes are the real monsters she tells you
she pulls you in for a hug
a warm one that smells like chamomile and
chocolate
her forehead on your own
she looks deep into your eyes
and you see pain and anger
you see a dark temple
hands sliding on marble pillars

you see horrible understanding and terror
but also overflowing love

and you know
she will sit with you on this couch for centuries
to take away your pain
she will give your own snakes
and glowing green eyes
she will teach you to sculpt
without touching a thing
she will hold you fiercely and tightly when you
need to cry

I know too many women who have visited
Medusa
not for her tea
not for her warmth
not for her cozy, bookshelf lined cottage
but to arm themselves against the unspeakable
to find comfort and solace and protection
to get snakes of their own with teeth and poison
and fangs

and to turn monsters masquerading as men to
stone

Eos

Eos I'm so sorry
seduced was I by the nymphs of the evening
Hesperides dancing in streaks of gold
dusk's embers fading to inky blackness
I once believed the sun in her setting more
stunning than you
rosy-fingered titaness, I watched your sisters
trail lackluster across the sky
and mistook it for art

I held too tight to my slumber
burrowed snug into morphean dreams
I traded your splendor for lulling darkness
I might have spent forever fooled
I might have never laid new eyes on you
but he prefers the sunrise

your sisters fill the heavens with dark blotches
patches of shadowed clouds
calmly they are laid to rest under blankets of
stars
slipping into their mother's silent embrace
but you

O Eos you're a glowing line on the horizon that
explodes into our night
you're full of burning reds and soft oranges
all slid atop each other like lovers
your hands claw across the sky
leaving haloed clouds and shimmering threads in
their wake
Nyx's star-flecked blanket is flung away
with violence, you do not burst silently forth
I can hear you roaring from the earth below

I sit and watch
seeing one out of a pitifully small handful of
your masterpieces
and I believe him
but Eos, my favorite sunrise of all time is us

you painted a rising dawn between our ribs
one full of hot burning reds, blazing between us
homer says you have saffron robes
and you must have sewn them into my cheeks
with flushing warmth and down cast lashes
you laid soft oranges in his eyes
when he smiles at me I see them: calm, and
subtle, and breathtaking
you took your time creating us, hiding the sun in
our curves and dimples
threading energy and burning love into every
moment

one hand on the wheel, the other tracing light
circles on my palm
I smile through the words of his favorite song
and I'm suddenly staring at the sun—fully risen
and painfully bright

our sunrise is a beginning, like all sunrises are
it's a hesitant promise
the dawn of a life
who knows if we'll have a sunset
but what I do know is this: our sunset would be
just as spectacular as our sunrise
and Eos, I wouldn't regret a glowing inch of the
whole day

Artemis

I see the moonlit huntress everyday
vibrant and violent
a divine feminine
a beauty loud and strong
full and angry
resilient and unshattered

she walks among us in our womanhood
present in the arch of a neck, thrown back in
uninhibited laughter
she is the moonlight draping itself upon white
smiles and stumbling heels on a city street
her huntresses crowd bar bathrooms, sinking
into familiarity and love
they are no strangers
connected with a thundering bowstring
chest to chest, protection and adoration pouring
between them
smiling at one another in filmy mirrors
exclamations of beauty tinkle around dingy
wallpaper
like shards of moonlight

I see her in the wild abandon of youth
glowing silver in the eyes of little girls

racing up trees and smirking down their trunks
at mortal boys below
I see her marching in the ranks of activists
brandishing their signs like spear points
messages scrawled murderously in red
no silence and no forgiveness
they prowl with the disdain of a vengeful
goddess
I see her in every curve and plane of women
bodies gorgeously and wonderfully rendered
stunning compositions unique and
goddess-blessed with beauty and strength

I feel her in the press of a wrist on a temple
a cool breath on a forehead
the intimate quiet and focus of make up
application
a sacred and holy rite
artful war paint applied
gingerly and purposefully
the sweep of eyeliner arrow sharp and intense
a dusting of highlighter along a cheekbone like
stars settling on an upturned face

women are soul made blood and bone
feeling things wildly and fearlessly
they have pain and love and anger folded into
their hips
capable of empathy and hatred

grief and ecstasy
born from a forest glowing with moonlight
Prometheus molded men
but Artemis drew women in the stars

Persephone

a flutter of pink cotton
arms loose around his waist
leather warm on her cheek
steady hum and glinting metal beneath
open and cloudless sky above
freedom echos down the gravel
flowing over her skin mixed with warm summer
air
and she thinks
this underworld is the brightest thing she's ever
seen

he kisses her fingers wrists and ankles
leaving bands of jewels in his wake
until she's dripping in luxury
glittering like the night sky
he never says her name
flowers fall from his lips instead
messy with nectar and sticking to her skin
poppy
orchid
iris
lily
she presses open their shapes
immortalizing every stem and curve

and now their ink climbs from her wrists to her
shoulders
down her ribs and hips
twining her knuckles and toes
the vibrance of spring time
his mural across her body

his kisses are sick sweet
like cherry candy
his mouth swollen and the deep red color
of pomegranate seeds
she spends her nights in wonder
atop a dark king's sheets
floating through pleasure
and awestruck by love
she does not miss the sameness and boredom
of cut and pasted green lawns
suburban goddess
on a throne of perfectly pruned peonies
but she prefers unruly rose beds
and a man of petal and thorn
leather and metal
escape and freedom

she thinks
mama forgive me
for courting death like a lover
and loving his darkness like an old friend
but I cannot control myself

wrapped in him
and drugged on pomegranate kisses
I lay in transition
like the spring's thawing before summer heat
a dawn and a dusk
a girl and a woman
innocent and defiled

call him Hades
and me Persephone

Circe

hazy scenes
muddled in memory and time
youth was vague
like trying to watch a movie while falling asleep
nothing stuck longer than a moment
until there's an bundle in my small arms
wrinkled red with eyes squeezed shut
screaming her way into to the world
more strength in her tiny lungs
than any mortal should have
a baby Circe, with the the power of an
enchantress glowing within her

blazing through existence
little Circe grew beside me
as we stumbled through our life
taming the lions and climbing the cliffs
never farther than a hands breadth away
I sit at her side through all
acolyte and protector
companion and teacher
with the adoration of sisterhood
tightly occupying this heart
I don't feel large enough

to contain this love
my mortal frame insufficient
too tame a host for olympian powers

have I told her lately?
that she holds magic within her?
writhing power and strength thundering in her
heart
with sparks flying from her smile
lightning clashing in her eyes
setting rooms alight with ease and grace
have I told her lately that pride is too paltry a
word
for what fills my chest when I look upon the
woman she has become
an enchantress, a goddess alive within her
Circe has grown up
and I watch her face down the world
capable and magical as the day she was born

Ariadne

sand shifts beneath me
once grand curling seashells
pulverized into a fine grit
bleached edges look like mossy bones
tapping dully together
they scatter underfoot
crushing and ceaseless
the salt water rages with masculine anger and
passion
crystal blue wrath and violence spilling onto the
shore

son of the sea
your eyes were not so cold when I first beheld
them
O Theseus, your eyes were made of tranquil
waters
your smile sunbeams refracted across the
rippling surface
no wind and rain, no roaring waves
just a peaceful soul calling out to my own
reaching out on a deceitful tide
pulling me toward you
pulling me further from home

where deeper and untamed waters lie
I watched you shed your tropical beach for stone
cliffs and shrieking winds

I stumble further into the foam
cold splashing up my calves haphazard and
messy
I'm desperate to leave the seashells
disgusted by the weakness of the shore
she who remains still, awaiting abuse
accepting mistreatment
drowning in his enormity
I know her story too well

the sea reaches my face
though I stand only thigh-deep
salt water traces my cheeks and neck
replacing his hands and lips
warmth turned cold and echoing
mocking ghostly hands of memory
more painful than a physical blow
give me Daedalus and rumbling metal walls
give me bloodthirsty and horned brother
give me shamed mother in high towers
anything but dreaded Naxos
where ghosts wander
memories waiting to tear out my chest
sip happiness from my heart like wine
until I'm left a hollow flask

drained and wraith-like haunting these beaches

I trace the stretching blurred horizon
habit and denial cold fingers on my chin
forcing my gaze up
to where your ship disappeared long ago
carried away on your father's rolling might
you streamed through my fingers like sea water
I should've known better than to hold you
the fickle golden ichor of the gods runs through
your veins

so cold am I
leached of feeling and love
so empty
so hopeless
so aching I almost do not feel it
I almost do not feel the heat behind me
a heat that feels like sunshine
different from the vast and distant beams of the
open ocean
spreading across my back
I feel the kind of sun that filters through forest
canopies
and falls to trace playfully along waving grass
beds
a summer breeze ruffles my skirts
quiet and gentle
heavy with moisture

it smells like grapes and fresh bread
it sounds like a flute lazily fluttering through the
air
eyes closed I do not turn
I cling to my imagined summer among the trees
I beg it not to fall away like yet another ship on
the horizon

my feet leave the churning water below
the warmth becomes two arms
banded beneath my hips and pulling me up into
the air
I'm looking no longer at the sea
but two smiling eyes of deep brown
a tumble of unruly curls
falling forward off of his broad face to swing in
the air between us
he is joy and boyish mischief
relaxation and madness

I no longer feel cold
and I never look towards the horizon again

Cassandra

not a soul believes you
when you scream
our world is ending
you yell into the void of humanity
and watch us follow a future of destruction and
death
as we tumble into gaping space
off of the cliff you saw all along

you gaze out and see
mother gaia crying
wilting leaves and oil slicked oceans
crumbling glaciers and rising tides
raging fires and swirling hurricanes
down her cheeks
streams polluted waters
aching wounds plunged into her breast
mankind treats her bounty as they do any other
woman
her unconsenting body as their own property
her cries as false
her retaliation as unthreatening

Cassandra you see it
the death of all that we know

fast approaching on a black carriage of our own
design
cursed to be alone in your visions of doom
scoffed at by those you try to save
and with your warnings of peril loftily ignored
we plow further into oblivion
Troy falling to rubble at our feet
Agamemnon's troops surging toward us
at a breakneck and unstoppable pace

you've seen worlds destroyed
torn to shreds by man and his hubris
time and time again we fall
you'll sit back, to watch another rendition of the
same dance
of ignorance and irresponsibility
careless and reckless in our supposed progress
and you'll remain
millennia from now
to see others repave our steps into darkness
still deaf to your echoing cries

Adonis

burgundy blood grows slowly
on a bed of grass
deep red satin draping leisurely
across the forest floor
a beautiful demigod
with a soul of golden light
slowly leaking out
dimming eyes and paling face

clasped tightly in goddess arms
clinging to his fragile mortal life
desperate and helpless
to stem the flow of loss
growing in a scarlet pool at her knees
staining linen memories
ruby red pain seeping through time

his frame
once capable and seeming immortal
lies limp and empty
drops of sea foam tears
anointing his temples and the bridge of his nose

losing something beautiful and heaven-sent
the peaks of Olympus seem to quake

in the shockwaves of emptiness
there is a silence and an acknowledgment
of the terrible
of the inevitable
as something unique and breathtaking
slips away forever

Medea

Jason gives Medea bruises
like bouquets of flowers every evening
He carries them home from work in his fists
Pressed against the muscles of his chest
Brushing the lapels of his suit
To deliver them
Petal-purple on her cheeks and ribs
Violets and tulips under her blushed and
swelling skin

Medea counts her bruises every night
cloaked in darkness and egyptian cotton sheets
the bruises she tallies are relief and thankfulness
so long as the purple he paints doesn't splatter
her children
she'll be a canvas if the artist's eye doesn't trace
their young limbs

Medea hears a whimper filter under the kitchen
door
knowing fills her skull
pressing ice to a small, tearful eye
the knowing seeps down her cheeks
smoothing wispy hair back over a tiny
shuddering shoulder

the knowing hitches in her lungs

O Medea, you give your children melatonin and
benadryl
and lay their limp bodies upon a coffee table
pyre
with shaking hands you smear jagged steaks of
your blood on their mouths and necks
a curated murder scene

O Medea, you tug your hair out of its ponytail
the one Jason loves
and allow chunks of brown curls to fall
haphazard and free
to brush your delicate shoulders
so mussed you'd only allow it when love-drunk
and sweaty
you apply red lipstick in your vanity mirror
artfully smudged
one corner pulled down to your chin
a curated affair

O Medea, you wait until the headlights trace the
ceiling
and Jason comes striding into the house
his angry eyes already afire
land on the double-scene staged before him
with the spirit of old Hollywood starlets within
you

and weight of your children's lives on your
shoulders
you become a villainess, pulling the linen mask
over your face
a gleefully murderous smile plastered on
a shroud of malevolence tugged into place

O Medea, you spin a tale so somber and
macabre
that the world detests you
but Medea, you escaped with your children
and you have stayed hidden under the veil of
their hatred
never to be seen again

Hercules

not every little girl has a Hercules
12 labors prove too much
men fall from pedestals
one by one
plummet reflected in shining youthful eyes

hydras rage on
unchecked poison
seeping from jagged maws
I watched daughters stand alone
in a world of mythic beasts
sharp talons slashing through defenses of glass
shattering at any contact

but I stand in this battlefield
unthreatened by daunting existence as a woman
no naivety holds me
in diamond cages of gild
because Hercules puts swords in my hands
he straps leather armor to my chest
he drapes Nemean skins on my shoulders
tawny hide protection
from spear or sneer
a callused hand, club strong on my shoulder
trains a young woman

in respect, defense, and security
arms her in daggers made of stone and
confidence
she stands stronger than the Cretan Bull
and stares down any horned challenger
with the poise and aloofness of a demigod

I've watched fatherhood rot
falling prematurely from blackened limbs
but my Hercules glows vibrant and strong
loving and stable
as golden as the Hesperides apple
I can only pray I fall close to his tree

Aphrodite

you must have smirked down at me
seashells twined in your hair
pearls polished on your collarbones
dripping down to your waist
your glowing silhouette
elegant and refined

you must have scoffed with Cupid
rolled your eyes at my expense
as I stood in front of all
and declared myself content
as I went on about freedom
confidence at the start of a new life
poised to plunge forward
gleefully alone and celebrating it

unaware and unassuming
I issued a challenge that echoed through
Olympus
to land in your eager ear
prideful goddess you are
as vengeful as you are beautiful
I know that you set to work straight away
plucking him from my past
like a pearl from it's shelled slumber

molding him from sea foam and passion
in your image you made him divine and
stunning
with a heart as deep as the sea
and a mind carved from Hephaestus' depths
perfect and mine
you placed him casually and innocently in my
path

you must have smirked down at me
seashells and pearls glittering with mischief
as I fumbled and fell
out of control
heart bleeding in my hands
for the very first time
helplessly in love and terrified at what that
meant
blessed am I you were merciful that day
and etched me into his heart as well
the fall wasn't followed
by anticipated painful impact
I am chastened yet happy
with your lesson thoughtfully received
I won't be so quick to challenge you again

you may have smirked down at me
or maybe it was a fond smile
at a headstrong girl not sold on love
about to eat her words

Patroclus

a war-torn battlefield
a decade spent knee deep
in mud and misery
damage carved into the soil
the walls of Troy loom above
casting shadows upon us like spells
bathing our writhing mass in darkness
as if we deserve the sunlight
our violence and bloodlust belong only in realms
of grey
to hades we go and to hades we send others
the lives of men sent seeping down
through Trojan muck
on their journey to judgement
and a dark king's throne room

Achilles' armor too large
a shell of demigod strength
floating above mortal limbs
I push forward
and another spear thrusts through a neck
I know not his name nor his heart
but with precision
cold and unfaltering
I bury both

for what purpose and for whose sake
but the pride of an angry king
coveting a lost queen
at the price of Trojan lives and Greek humanity

Hector spots my glimmering disguise
mistakes my gore cloaked skin
for Thetis' glowing Nereid tan
and begins to stalk a path through the carnage
the son of Priam mere inches away
I see my death clearly displayed
like a string of clouds on the dawn horizon
and as Hector's spear brushes my chest
coy and teasing as a lover
gains entry to my heart and pierces it through
as my breath slides out of me
sighing and gentle
I know Ares is not finished with us

his gleeful rage echoes
his battlefield stretches miles
his greed winds into the hearts of nations
fading away I see bloodied dunes of sand
a forest of rain and vines smelling like metal and
fear
I see open rolling hills of corpses
I see wars that have yet to be waged

and I know this world will be his bleeding alter

with men carrying anger in their hearts like
spears
and mistaking themselves heroes

Calypso

country calypso
Odysseus couldn't stay long
and in his rippling wake he left
a broken heart
and a pair of pudgy cheeks
with his smile and your eyes

before departing your shores
for Ithaca and hidden Penelope
unknowing he preserved memories
froze your fleeting summer in amber
staining sepia a lake-side picnic
a rope swing and a plunge
into cold water and warm passion
sandy toes and sunburned shoulders
pressed together under oak canopies
lazily falling in love the way only children can

but your paradise was a pause
in his hero's journey across the world
you're an adventure and a dalliance
a supporting character in the epic they'll sing
one day
a cautionary tale about who to love

he leaves you as carelessly as he loved you

now you hold your chin high
in grocery stores and coffee shops
against whispers about your curse
they gossip with dripping disdain
venom-viscous words pierce your back
calypso is trapped in Ogygia
her island beaches sandy nets
keep her stuck and unmoving
with a baby boy on her hip
poor thing
bless her whore heart

your nymph spirit and large heart aren't wasted
on this town
odysseus may have left
but he gave you the love of your life
O calypso you love your son more than anything
in this world
summer memories become foggy and fond
for love is not youthful lust and naive promises
but the all-consuming compassion of
motherhood
you raise him on sunshine and cloudless skies
he grows up in crystal waters
and leafy green trees
dodging their trunks
you play pirates and cowboys with him

country calypso and her baby boy live happily
ever after
content in each other's company
and all the better
than cursed Odysseus
and his tragic fate

Narcissus

flower boy
sees flower boy
a reflection of himself
rendered perfectly in another
not a flaw to be seen
blooming prettily at the waters edge

narcissus meet the pool
your petals look even softer on him
more pearly
more vibrant against the rest of the world
your leaves unfurl
plump and delicate and vulnerable
with every wall lowered
he reflects your reveal
bouncing your bleeding heart back at you
until you lean close enough to touch
to kiss and hold
to bury yourself in him

the water ripples
for a moment he distorts
scales and perspective change
his stem is sharp and bloodied
his pollen toxic

a smile is a sneer
a hug turned chokehold

frightening and sudden
you reel back
and slip

into the pool you slide
silent and almost docile
without warning enough to scream
drowning in him
you sink to the murky bottom

petals askew
you breathe no more

Pollux

call them castor and pollux
with stars binding them together
two sisters trample night's velvet underfoot
dizzy with laughter
clutching for breath
immortalized and fleeting all at once

soulmates tracing their way across diamond
skies
they left the heavens
and poured themselves into bodies
starlight and solar-flares made human
standing stable hand in hand
children of the gods and of reaching night sky
touching earth for a brief lifetime

the intimacy of a shared life
of nights spent whispering over pillowcases
and days spent weaving imaginations into one
I know them because we are them
and while life's path isn't certain
I know I'll leave as I began:
by your side
back to the stars we'll return

Icarus

when the sun is such a pleasant warmth
it's easy to sidle up too close
without realizing you're in danger of falling
we often forget that Icarus fell
one feather at a time

I too was escaping Crete
on wings constructed of my past
and in the beams of afternoon sunlight
I lost feathers and only felt lighter

my descent began subtly
with burgers sitting half eaten
in paper boxes beneath us
as we wondered at a shared childhood
nostalgia coating our laughs like wax
a feather snapped away in the wind
leaving me none the wiser

an evening looking up at the stars
and writing our own constellations
the rocks beneath us were hard
and the ocean wind was cold
but our smiles stayed firmly in place
as another feather floated away

mornings spent lying still
with a guitar balanced on our chests
you played me your favorite songs
and showed off by learning mine
you reached out apollo-blessed fingers
and plucked a feather from my wings
tossing it carelessly away
and even if I had seen
I might not have cared
so lost in your music was I

windy bluffs and winding cliff roads
under a melting sunset
you held my hand and dove into freezing teal
water
without hesitation and just because I wanted to
and emerging from the water with shouts of
alarm
another feather was whisked way in the pacific
tide

with long calls stretching across a nation
and airport reunions reminiscent of hallmark
movies
my feathers molted away with every purple
night I spent missing you
and after a stumbling walk down bourbon street
sticky heels thumping cobblestone

the penultimate feather fluttered into the sun

to leave me sitting beside you
on a rainy fire escape
the showering sparks of fireworks reflecting in
our eyes
and their shuddering booms echoing in my chest
I clutched my very last feather
and hurled it into the puddled and foggy streets
of Boston
to fall chaotically and happily in love with you

Icarus would be proud

Daphne

I reject the laurel
I won't put your leaves in my hair
since he stole that too
in praising Apollo and his victory
they subjugate and possess you
in your desperate fleeing
you sacrificed your freedom
no longer visceral in form
you gave up flesh and limb
for leaves and roots
to maintain autonomy and choice

and yet
he plucked your leaves
poor imitation of your flowing locks
and at his groping and irreverent hands
what little left of you remains
has been commodified
and taken under his sunny mantle

so daphne
though your leaves are delicate and beautiful
I will not put them in my hair
they signify man's selfish coveting
of bodies they do not deserve to lust after

and your loss at his gain
his victories celebrated with crowns made of you
I reject his reclamation of your body
and comfort myself knowing
he will never have your soul

your leaves will never brush my head
instead I'll splash in shallow water
I'll swim in roaring rapids
and sigh your name like a prayer
under the rushing whisper of a waterfall
I'll be every bit the water nymph you were
and move my legs when you cannot
hug my sister and mother
while your arms lie tightly bundled in bark

and daphne
with every apollo I meet
I will rip your laurels from his crown
with your name on my lips
and your spirit in my eyes

Thisbe

face pressed against the screen
the buzzing static of a lagging call
rests on my skin
a sorry replacement for your touch
the simple press of a hug
a hand casually clasping mine
a light arm sweeping around my waist

warmth and comfort vanish
you are all glass and blue-lit pixels
your face a flat and flickering mirage
are you real if I cannot touch you?

the thisbe to my pyramus
I peer through a glowing tunnel
stretching mere inches and miles toward you
smiles and tears, laughs and sobs
all filter through our tiny portal
words of affection passed through the
immovable wall
back and forth we go

be safe
I love you
be safe

I miss you
please please please be safe

a lion stalks the perimeters of our walls
tawny paws swiping in 6 foot arcs
at the distance we've erected
danger and pain and death surround us
grateful
we should be grateful for this wall, and our
glowing tunnel
the safety in our separation
the unity in our isolation

one day we'll take the walls down
our fear vanishing softly like a fading screen
the calm black emptiness climbing slowly over
the edges
until just a dull obsidian mirror remains

but until then, I'll pretend
pretend I can climb right through the screen and
hold you
in staticy and lagging arms
press buzzing and humming kisses to your
cheeks
my Thisbe, glowing blue and beautiful through
the tiniest of holes

till we may touch again
x Pyramus